GIANTS HAVE US IN THEIR BOOKS

José Rivera

BROADWAY PLAY PUBLISHING INC
224 E 62nd St, NY, NY 10065
www.broadwayplaypub.com
info@broadwayplaypub.com

GIANTS HAVE US IN THEIR BOOKS:
SIX NAIVE PLAYS
© Copyright 1997 by José Rivera

All rights reserved. This work is fully protected under the copyright laws of the United States of America. No part of this publication may be photocopied, reproduced, stored in a retrieval system, or transmitted, in any form or by any means, electronic, mechanical, recording, or otherwise, without the prior permission of the publisher. Additional copies of this play are available from the publisher.

Written permission is required for live performance of any sort. This includes readings, cuttings, scenes, and excerpts. For amateur and stock performances, please contact Broadway Play Publishing Inc. For all other rights also please contact the author c/o B P P I.

First published by B P P I: December 1997
First printing, this edition: June 2014
Second printing: June 2015

I S B N: 978-0-88145-594-6

Book design: Marie Donovan
Typeface: Palatino
Printed and bound in the U S A

CONTENTS

Plays by the Author .... *iv*
Dedication .... *vi*
Notes .... *vii*
Original production .... *viii*

ACT ONE

FLOWERS 1
TAPE 13
A TIGER IN CENTRAL PARK 21

ACT TWO

GAS 35
THE CROOKED CROSS 43
THE WINGED MAN 61

PLAYS

THE HOUSE OF RAMON IGLESIA (1983)
THE PROMISE (1988)*
EACH DAY DIES WITH SLEEP (1990)*
MARISOL (1992)
TAPE (1993)*
FLOWERS (1994)*
CLOUD TECTONICS (1995)*
MARICELA DE LA LUZ LIGHTS THE WORLD
GODSTUFF
THE STREET OF THE SUN (1996)
GIANTS HAVE US IN THEIR BOOKS (1997)*
SUEÑO (1998)
LOVERS OF LONG RED HAIR (2000)
REFERENCES TO SALVADOR DALÍ MAKE ME HOT (2000)*
SONNETS FOR AN OLD CENTURY (2000)*
ADORATION OF THE OLD WOMAN (2002)*
SCHOOL OF THE AMERICAS (2006)*
MASSACRE (SING TO YOUR CHILDREN) (2007)*
BRAINPEOPLE (2008)*
BOLEROS FOR THE DISINCHANTED (2008)
HUMAN EMOTIONAL PROCESS (2008)
PABLO AND ANDREW AT THE ALTAR OF WORDS (2010)
GOLDEN (2010)
THE KISS OF THE SPIDER WOMAN *(translation)* (2010)

THE HOURS ARE FEMININE (2011)
LESSONS FOR AN UNACCUSTOMED BRIDE (2011)
THE BOOK OF FISHES (2011)
WRITTEN ON MY FACE (2012)
ANOTHER WORD FOR BEAUTY (2013)
THE LAST BOOK OF HOMER (2013)
THE GARDEN OF TEARS AND KISSES (2014)
SERMON FOR THE SENSES (2014)
CHARLOTTE (2014)

*published & licensed for the stage by B P P I

For Adena and Teo

NOTES

One day I was talking to my then four-year-old daughter Adena about fairy-tale stories and imaginary creatures like witches and giants. She wanted to know where they came from. I told her they came from people making them up and putting them in their books. She thought about this a second and said, "Oh. Then giants have us in their books." The following are six short plays written as if we were the subject of stories told by giants.

The play can be produced with between six and twenty actors. Some characters are more archetypal than actual—so characters like VISITOR, NO NAME, and the TIGER can be played by either sex. Characters like FOOGMAN and VISITOR can be played by any race. CHEO in GAS must be Latino. KATHY in the CROOKED CROSS should be Jewish. If possible, always push for ethnic diversity.

GIANTS HAVE US IN THEIR BOOKS: SIX NAIVE PLAYS received its world premiere at the Magic Theatre (Mame Hunt, Artistic Director; Albert Hasson, Managing Director) on 9 November 1993, with the following cast and creative contributors:

    Sean San José Blackman
    Michael Girardin
    Margo Hall
    Dennis Matthews
    Selena Navarro
    Michelle Pelletier
    Megan Blue Stermer

Director .... Roberto Gutierrez Varea
Set design .... Lauren Elder
Lighting design .... Jeff Rowlings
Costume design .... Chrystene Ells
Sound design .... J A Deane
Stage manager .... Lisa Lance
Production assistant .... Susan Murdoch
Assistant director .... Antigone Trimis

FLOWERS

CHARACTERS & SETTING

LULU
BETO

TIME

The present

PLACE

LULU's *bedroom. Echo Park, California.*

(Echo Park, California. A bedroom.)

*(*BETO*, a boy of ten, is sitting on the floor.* LULU*, a girl of twelve, his sister, is sitting up in bed, looking at a mirror.* BETO *is playing a hand-held video game. There are red spots on* LULU*'s face.)*

LULU: I don't understand. Why does this have to happen to me?

BETO: You're cursed.

LULU: Today of all days.

BETO: Bad karma. You were a slave driver in a former life.

LULU: My life is over!

BETO: It's not so bad. You're just about to become the ugliest girl in your school.

LULU: Shut up. You're not helping.

BETO: All people will shun you.

LULU: But what does it mean? Does it mean something? Is it a message to me from some eternal power somewhere that can't communicate in normal ways so it must find a way to signal me that's more direct, if more undecipherable and mysterious?

BETO: Lulu, it's zits.

LULU: I *know* it's zits.

BETO: So what's the philosophical questioning about?

LULU: It's about *meaning*, butthead. It's about me. This didn't happen to Fefu or Migdalia or Nelly, it happened to me. That means something.

BETO: That you're self-obsessed.

LULU: Was I bad? Did I think an unholy thought recently?

BETO: Pimples are just a hormone thing, you know, you're becoming a woman.

LULU: I've been a woman. I know about hormones. But these zits happened today, on my twelfth birthday, all full blown, no warning, nothing, a complete and total coup d'etat. Like an announcement of some kind. A proclamation.

BETO: You're dreaming.

LULU: *(Quiet, frightened)* And—and—Beto—they're all in this weird pattern, too. I don't understand it. I'm turning totally hideous!

BETO: Maybe they say something if you can read them backwards.

LULU: Just pure ugliness on *my* face!

BETO: Use Oxyscrub. That ends it.

LULU: I tried. I did. I've been scrubbing all day. It doesn't help. These bastards are tenacious. They cling. They feast on the oils of my face. They multiply and laugh their heads off!

BETO: You're sick.

LULU: And there's something...you know I've been around zits. Zits and I are no strangers. It's one of the benefits of seventh grade: you get awfully familiar with the anatomy of pimples. These guys...are different. They really are. Their shape. Their size. Their texture. Like it's a new strain of zits. A separate species that's found fertile ground on my face. And, like, I'm this carrier of this new race of pimples, like a genetic mutation evolution thing, I'm serious.

BETO: God!

LULU: Look at them and you'll see for yourself.

BETO: No, thanks. You're just plain weird, Lulu.

(BETO *freezes.* LULU *speaks to the audience.*)

LULU: He can laugh. He doesn't know. Things don't just happen to me that mean nothing. I'm not just a girl. I'm something else. A signal. A preface. What happens to me has big importance. I just know it. I don't care if nobody else does!

(LULU *leaves.* BETO *unfreezes and speaks to the audience.*)

BETO: Some people can't get out of themselves. They're stuck in their personalities. It's a life sentence. It's horrible to watch. But you can't do much about it. My sister Lulu's of that ilk. She can't have a normal experience. Somehow, some way, she thinks the universe speaks through her. That cosmic truths are resonating through her bones. That Gods of ancient civilizations are obsessed with the way she walks. It's a pain in the ass, frankly. Who needs it? I want to eat hot food and slide into second base with my pals. I want silence when I sleep and a set of parents who respect each other enough. Just enough. These are not cosmic concerns. I know I'm a slug. I'm not a goddess. My sister is a goddess. There's responsibility there, being the brother of a goddess. But frankly I don't think I'm up to it.

(LULU *comes back on. The zits on her face have mutated.* LULU *now has long, thin, green tubes, six inches long, growing out of her face. They are very ugly and strange.* LULU *is in shock.*)

LULU: I'm about to scream.

(BETO *looks at her.*)

BETO: Holy shit.

LULU: Do you see what's going on here?

BETO: Is this some kind of trick?

LULU: Does it look like a trick? I've got tubes! Tubes of flesh are growing out of my face! It's a nightmare!

BETO: I've never seen anything like this, Lulu. Did you tell Mom and Dad?

LULU: No. I'm afraid they'll think I'm on drugs or something.

BETO: Puberty's really grabbed you by the throat, girl!

LULU: It's not puberty, Beto. I'm telling you. I can feel it. There's some other force at work here. If it's puberty, it's not the puberty everyone else knows about.

BETO: Have you tried using—?

LULU: I've tried everything. There isn't a medicine in the bathroom that hasn't found its way to my face. I've put Borax on my face. I've put motor oil. Detergent.

BETO: Maybe it's an allergic reaction.

LULU: You have to go to the drugstore and bring back everything you can get your hands on. I'm serious. I'm worried. Steal if you have to.

BETO: I'll do it. I'll steal for you.

(BETO *runs off.* LULU *is close to tears. She speaks to the audience.*)

LULU: I am going to be known as the ugliest girl on the West Coast. That's the meaning of these marks. This is punishment for my vanity! Just as I turn twelve and enter beautiful womanhood with eyes and lips and hips and tits. It's God's way of telling me I've spent my energies in the wrong way! Okay, Supreme Being! I've learned my lesson! Call off the dogs!

(LULU *exits crying.* BETO *runs back on, a bag in his hands. He speaks to the audience.*)

BETO: I've never shoplifted before, but my sister is worth it. I'm energized with a new purpose in life. This is extraordinary. Is it possible I'm growing up too? That she and I—mortal enemies since the moment of my conception—are somehow sharing the same growth hormones, somehow experiencing, by the secretion of some Super Pituitary Gland somewhere, a kind of joint puberty? So every new thought in her head resonates in mine? Each new stretch of muscle, each new hair follicle, is both mine and hers, like we were some kind of Siamese combination, ever sympathetic, ever united? I kinda hope so. I never understood her. She never let me. I always felt I was missing something. But now this crisis has united us. I feel for me. Amazing. Am I going crazy? Naw. I'm not. I'm part of her now. We're together. *(Smiles)* How very cool. How very advanced of me.

(LULU *comes back on. Her face has now broken out in large beautiful tropical flowers, like hibiscus.* BETO *looks at her and drops his bag.)*

LULU: Hi.

(Beat)

BETO: I don't believe it.

LULU: Every morning brings a surprise.

BETO: Those are flowers.

LULU: Hibiscus to be exact.

BETO: They're growing out of your face, Lulu!

LULU: You're an uncanny observer of life. MY FACE IS TURNING INTO A PLANT! I'M GOING TO COMMIT SUICIDE! *(She pulls huge hedge clippers from her back pocket and puts them to her throat.)*

BETO: You can't do this, Lulu!

LULU: Yeah, why not? Do you see what I've become? I'm a horror movie. I'm a late-night, black-and-white B-flick about mutation! I'VE BECOME FUCKING BOTANICAL!

BETO: You're a miracle! You're—

LULU: I'm the front page of next week's *Inquirer!* "Twelve-Year-Old Suburban Girl Turns Into Human Flowerbed." I'm a monster. I'm a curse. God hates me. He truly hates me. He's marked me in some despicable way. I've been punished now, and there's no point in living anymore.

(LULU *tries to cut her throat with the hedge clippers.* BETO *stops her. She looks at him, tears in her eyes.*)

BETO: But—but—but—it's kinda...beautiful.

(LULU *puts the hedge clippers down.*)

LULU: Beautiful?

BETO: Yeah. Really. In a deep, cool way. Lyrical.

LULU: This?

BETO: I know you don't see it. But look. Look at the way they curve. They grow magnificently out of the topsoil of your face. They radiate some kind of unearthly beauty, Lulu, they really do. You should consider yourself lucky.

LULU: I consider myself a freak. A leper. No. My life is effectively over. There's not much for me to do. I could get surgery. But they'll probably grow back. I could wear a mask the rest of my life, but it's hard to grow up that way and do the things they say you're supposed to do, like get married and have children. No. Only death will relieve me.

(LULU *raises the hedge clippers to her throat. We hear a swarm of bees outside.*)

LULU: What's that?

BETO: Bees.

LULU: Bees?

BETO: They've come to pollinate you.

LULU: God, you're mocking me! You're having a laugh at my expense! Is this why I was created?!

BETO: Lulu, please, I don't think you should kill yourself. This is really a cool thing that's happened to you. Use it. Exploit it. There might be some incredible moral reward waiting for you.

LULU: BEES WANT TO FUCKING FERTILIZE THE STAMENS ON MY FACE, YOU IDIOT, WHAT THE HELL ARE YOU TALKING ABOUT??!?!?

(LULU *throws the hedge clippers on the ground and stomps off. The bee sounds die down.* BETO *speaks to the audience.*)

BETO: I can't tell her this, but I'm excited. I feel like I'm present at some uncanny turning point in the evolution of man. That my dear, homely, unexceptional sister has become the agent of some behemoth change about to be unleashed on the world. A firestorm of new ideas and enigmas. She. Her. That brat. That girl. That dear Lulu.

LULU: *(Off)* Help me. Help me quick!

(BETO *runs off and comes back on, carrying* LULU. LULU *is encircled by vines; she has branches growing out of her arms and roots forming at the bottom of her feet. There are a few tiny leaves in her hair.*)

(BETO *puts* LULU *on the bed. He looks at her a long moment before he speaks.*)

BETO: This is a new turn.

LULU: It's not just my face, Beto. It's all of me.

BETO: *(Quiet, sad)* I. I. I'm blown away, Lulu.

(LULU *gives a sad laugh. Even her voice is slightly different.*)

LULU: It gets harder and harder to move every second. I can actually feel wood forming under my skin. My—my bones are softening. And there are, like, leaves growing where my hair should be. It's—it's not just a bad case of zits here. This is a phenomenon, little brother. I'm turning into a rain forest.

BETO: Oh, my poor sister.

LULU: But don't. Don't feel sorry. I like the sunlight more and more. Maybe there are advantages to being vegetable. The sun feeds me. I can feel it. I really can. My green skin is all abuzz now. It's very active. Like having a beehive on you all the time. Churning out new food, creating sugars out of pure light. It's really quite a feeling. I don't know how to describe it.

BETO: We have to stop this, Lulu.

LULU: I think my roots are searching for the bed. I'll probably intertwine with the bed real soon, then my roots will find the floor and burrow in and I'll be permanently attached to the earth. I won't be a mobile creature. I'll be rooted to the planet. I guess that's when I'll stop being fully animal. Everything I need will come to me: sunlight, water, air, fertilizer, insect life. If that happens, I will prosper. I may even live to bear fruit! You could bake me into a pie! You could plant my seeds all over Echo Park! You could decorate my branches on Christmas!... But, if those good things don't come to me, I will die. There is nothing I can do about it. A vegetable life is about waiting. Waiting to get the gifts of life or waiting perpetually for the end to come. The animal tension has ended for me. That's, that's a relief, I think. A plant is calm. Serene. Complete.

BETO: *(Crying)* Oh, my dear Lulu!

(The lights go to black. A pool of light comes up on another section of the stage. BETO *enters the pool of light.)*

BETO: I have to stop feeling sorry for myself. I will stop. I did stop when I started to realize something. That Lulu was no different than the rest of us. That she was being taken over by alien monster forces that pulled and pushed at her body in ways she couldn't control. But that's all of our fates, isn't it? And, for most, for most, that turning point brings you hair and breasts and balls that sag and a yearning for jerking off and then babies come and you get older, really older, like your mid-thirties, and your body changes more and more so that by the end you're really completely different anyway, unrecognizable. How different is that from turning into a plant like Lulu did? I figured something out. It's happened before. Other friends of hers. Friends of mine. Relatives. They disappear. There's hush-hush. And suddenly their family has a new fern growing out front. There's a point—one day you get to it—everybody does—you either turn to the right and become an animal, sexual being—or you simply, with no fanfare—you simply turn a slightly different direction, and nature takes you gently by the hand and puberty becomes the transformation into leaves and branches and roots and seeds and buds and bark. Nature simply says, "No, not you. I have something else in mind for you." *(A little scared)* I wonder what she's going to say to me.

(The lights up on the bed, now completely covered by vines and thick leaves. Roots sink into the earth. There is absolutely nothing left of LULU. BETO *looks at the exotic plant.)*

BETO: Lulu. The amazing.

(A leaf falls from the plant and lands at BETO's *feet.* BETO *picks up the leaf and looks at it. There's something on it. Words?* BETO *reads the leaf.)*

BETO: "Hey, little brother. Goodbye."

*(*BETO *drops the leaf. He goes off briefly and comes back with a watering can. He waters* LULU. *Black out.)*

END OF PLAY

TAPE

CHARACTERS & SETTING

VISITOR
NO NAME
VOICE

TIME

The present

PLACE

In a dark room

(*A small, dark room. No windows. One door. A* VISITOR *is being led in by* NO NAME. *In the room is a simple wooden table and a chair. On the table is a large reel-to-reel tape recorder, a glass of water, and a pitcher of water.*)

VISITOR: Fucking dark in here.

NO NAME: I'm sorry.

VISITOR: No, I know it's not your fault.

NO NAME: Those stupid lights...

VISITOR: What does it matter now?

NO NAME: ...not very bright.

VISITOR: Who cares?

NO NAME: We don't want to cause you any undue suffering. If it's too dark in here, I'll make sure one of the other attendants replaces the light bulb.

(*The* VISITOR *looks at* NO NAME.)

VISITOR: Any "undue suffering"?

NO NAME: That's right.

(*The* VISITOR *looks at the room.*)

VISITOR: Is this where I'll be?

NO NAME: That's right.

VISITOR: Will you be outside?

NO NAME: Yes.

VISITOR: The entire time?

NO NAME: The entire time.

VISITOR: Is it? Boring?

NO NAME: (*As if not understanding*) I'm sorry?

VISITOR: Is it boring?

NO NAME: *(Soft smile)* It's my job. It's what I do.

VISITOR: Oh. *(Beat)* Will I get anything to eat or drink?

NO NAME: Well, we're not really set up for that. Most visitors don't get hungry—so we don't have what you'd call a kitchen. But we can send out for things. Little things. Cold food. Soft drinks.

VISITOR: *(Hopefully)* Beer?

NO NAME: *(Shocked)* I hope you're joking!

VISITOR: Not even on special occasions like my birthday?

NO NAME: *(Thinking)* ...well...I guess, maybe, on your birthday.

VISITOR: *(Truly appreciative)* Great. Thanks.

(Beat)

NO NAME: Do you have any more questions before we start? Because, if you do, that's okay. It's okay to ask as many questions as you want. I'm sure you're very curious. I'm sure you'd like to know as much as possible, so you can figure out how it all fits together and what it all means and where you fit in. So please ask. That's why I'm here. Don't worry about the time. We have a lot of time.

(Beat)

VISITOR: I don't have any questions.

NO NAME: *(Disappointed)* You sure?

VISITOR: There's not much I really have to know, is there? Really?

NO NAME: No, I guess not. I just thought....

VISITOR: It's okay. I appreciate it. I know you're just trying to help. Make me feel better. I guess I really want to sit.

NO NAME: Sit.

(*The* VISITOR *sits on the chair and faces the tape recorder.*)

VISITOR: Okay, I'm sitting.

NO NAME: (*Hovering*) Is it...comfortable?

VISITOR: (*Exploding*) Jesus Christ! Does it matter? Does it really fucking matter if I'm comfortable or not?!

NO NAME: (*Pulling back*) No. I guess not.

(NO NAME *looks sad. The* VISITOR *looks at* NO NAME *and feels bad.*)

VISITOR: Hey, I'm sorry. I know it's not your fault. I'm being—don't know what I'm being—I'm sorry.

NO NAME: It's alright.

VISITOR: What's your name anyway? Do you have a name?

NO NAME: Not really. It's not allowed.

VISITOR: Really? Who says?

NO NAME: The rules.

VISITOR: You've actually seen these rules? They're in writing?

NO NAME: Oh, yes. *Everything's* in writing. Books! *Instructions* for everything. Laws, parables, examples, lessons—it's overwhelming sometimes—the *details*—that's why there's such a long and extensive training course.

VISITOR: (*Surprised*) There is?

NO NAME: Oh, yes. It's a *killer*—I mean, it's quite rigorous.

VISITOR: Shit.

NO NAME: You have to be a little bit of everything in my job. Confidant, confessor, friend, stern task master. Guide.

VISITOR: Guess that'd take a lot of time.

NO NAME: My teachers were great. They were strong and capable. They really pushed me. I was grateful. I knew I had been chosen for something unique and exciting. Something significant. I didn't mind the hard work and sleepless nights.

VISITOR: *(Surprised)* Oh? You sleep?

NO NAME: *(Smiles)* When I can.

(Beat)

VISITOR: Do you dream?

(Beat)

NO NAME: No. *(Beat)* That's not allowed.

(Beat)

VISITOR: I'm sorry.

NO NAME: It's something you get used to.

VISITOR: *(Trying to be chummy)* I know I went years without being able to remember one single dream I had. It really scared the shit out of me when I was ten and I just woke up and I had this dream about being chased by tigers in Central Park....

NO NAME: I know. I know that story. When you were ten. The tigers. The park.

VISITOR: Oh. Yeah. I guess you would know everything. Every story. Every secret.

NO NAME: *(Apologetic)* It's part of the training.
(A long uncomfortable silence.) Have you ever operated a reel-to-reel tape recorder before?

VISITOR: *(Suddenly terrified)* No, I haven't. I mean—no.

NO NAME: It's not hard. *(Demonstrates)* On here.

VISITOR: I, uhm, these things were pretty obsolete by the time I was old enough to afford stereo equipment, you know, I got into cassettes, 8-tracks, I mean I had this one copy of "Jesus Christ Superstar" I must've played a billion times, and, later, I got into C D's, but never one of these jobbies.

NO NAME: *(Demonstrates)* Off here. Play. Pause. Rewind.

VISITOR: *(Surprised)* Rewind?

NO NAME: In some cases the quality of the recording is so poor...you'll want to rewind it until you understand.

VISITOR: No fast forward?

NO NAME: Was that a joke?

VISITOR: *(Getting progressively more frightened)* It looks like a pretty good one! Sturdy! Is this the only tape?

(NO NAME laughs out loud—then quickly stops.)

NO NAME: No!

VISITOR: I didn't think so.

NO NAME: There are ten thousand boxes!

VISITOR: Ten thousand boxes? Did I really...did I really lie that much?

NO NAME: I'm afraid you did.

VISITOR: So...does everyone...go into a room like this?

NO NAME: Exactly like this. There's no differentiation. Everyone's equal.

VISITOR: For once!

NO NAME: What isn't equal, of course, is the amount of time you spend here. Listening.

VISITOR: *(Horror stricken)* Oh, God.

NO NAME: Listening, just to yourself. To your voice.

VISITOR: I know.

NO NAME: Listening, word by word, to every lie you ever told while you were alive.

VISITOR: Oh, God!

NO NAME: Every ugly lie to every person, every single time, every betrayal, every lying thought, every time you lied to yourself, deep in your mind, we were listening, we were recording, and it's all in these tapes, ten thousand boxes of them, in your own words, one lie after the next, over and over, until we're finished. So the amount of time varies. The amount of time you spend here all depends on how many lies you told. How many boxes of tape we have to get through together.

VISITOR: *(Almost in tears)* I'm sorry...

NO NAME: Too late.

VISITOR: I said I'm sorry! I said I'm sorry! I said it a million times! What happened to forgiveness?! I don't want to be here! I don't want this! I don't want to listen! I don't want to hear myself! I didn't mean to say the things I said! I don't want to listen!

NO NAME: Yes, well. Neither did we. Neither did we.

(NO NAME *looks sadly at the* VISITOR. NO NAME *turns on the tape recorder.* NO NAME *hits the "Play" button, the reels spin slowly, and the tape starts snaking its way through the machine.)*

(Silence)

(NO NAME *leaves the room, leaving the* VISITOR *all alone. The* VISITOR *nervously pours a glass of water.)*

(From the depths of the machine comes a long-forgotten voice.)

VOICE: "Where have you been? Do you know I've been looking all *over*? Jesus Christ! I went to Manny's! I went to the pharmacy! The school! I even called the police! Look at me, Jesus Christ, I'm *shaking*! Now look at me— look at me and tell me where the hell you were! Tell me right now!"

(Silence. As the VISITOR *waits, terrified and sad, for the lying response, the lights fade to black.)*

END OF PLAY

A TIGER IN CENTRAL PARK

CHARACTERS & SETTING

Actor
Oswald
Jennifer Leigh
Yvette
Tiger

TIME

The present

PLACE

Central Park, New York City

For Tim O'Gara

(Central Park, New York City. Day. An ACTOR *is holding up the sun.)*

*(*OSWALD *and* JENNIFER LEIGH *are building a tiger trap.)*

JENNIFER LEIGH: *(Frightened)* Oswald, I'm shaking! My God, isn't it amazing what the Fear of Death can do to a person?

OSWALD: *(Ditto)* To a person? To a whole city!

JENNIFER LEIGH: Imagine! Fear of this tiger has been enough to destroy an entire city's sex drive!

OSWALD: But if the trap works and we catch this tiger, Jennifer Leigh...the fear will end...and everyone will get their sex drives back! We'll be the heroes of Manhattan!

JENNIFER LEIGH: *(Looking at him)* Man, am I gonna make up for lost time. I can feel it already! You and me...a bottle of white wine...

OSWALD: *(Getting excited)* ...the old urge...

JENNIFER LEIGH: *(More excited)* ...our torsos... intertwining....

OSWALD: *(Ditto)* ...the sweet, fresh singing of our fingers...

JENNIFER LEIGH: ...the tearing, tiger *lust*...our screams of pleasure bouncing off the walls of the Upper West Side!

OSWALD: Stop! Stop! You're killing me!

*(*OSWALD *rushes at* JENNIFER LEIGH. *Terrified, she puts her hand up to stop him.)*

JENNIFER LEIGH: Not yet! Not until we finish the trap and catch the tiger!

(They finish building the tiger trap. They put in a bag marked "Tiger bait". They step back to admire their handiwork.)

JENNIFER LEIGH: We're gonna do it, Oswald. We're gonna do what thousands of policemen and scores of armed posses from the inner city, hunting day and night, couldn't

OSWALD: You really think?

JENNIFER LEIGH: I just don't get why so much manpower's been deployed...so many firearms...and yet this tremendous cat—eight hundred pounds of raw animal hunger, they say—is still out there...still free to pursue its single-minded, bloodthirsty dance of death...

OSWALD: Stop!

JENNIFER LEIGH: *(Getting into it)* ...pouncing silently on innocent children...emasculating whole subway lines...sucking on the bones of murdered Wall Street executives!

(She pounces on him, and he screams.)

OSWALD: I'm losing whatever residual horniness I had left!

(She gets off him.)

JENNIFER LEIGH: ...What's the *reason*? That's what I've never been able to figure out. I mean, a tiger that size can't just *hide*. It must have some kind of trick up its murderous sleeve. Some kind of magic. What could it be?

(YVETTE jogs by, upstage. JENNIFER LEIGH watches YVETTE jog away and gets an idea.)

JENNIFER LEIGH: I got it! This is a city of millions of *people*. It's the easiest city in the world to hide in...if you're a *person*.

OSWALD: Huh?

JENNIFER LEIGH: Notice? Our tiger stalks and feeds only at night. Why? Because...during the day...it's not a tiger...it's a person...

OSWALD: Wha'?

JENNIFER LEIGH: There's a legend from my childhood. A story we told only at night. In secret. About a tiger. He was an animal at night. And a person in the day. Like a werewolf.

OSWALD: *(Getting it)* But that means...the tiger could be anybody. It could be you, Jennifer Leigh.

JENNIFER LEIGH: Or you.

OSWALD: *(Panicking)* Yes, it could be me. Oh, my God. I feel terrible. All those innocent people!

JENNIFER LEIGH: Wait, no, it couldn't be you.

OSWALD: Really? I'm so happy.

JENNIFER LEIGH: Or me! The legend says...that people who turn into tigers at night have a certain mark on their faces. This mark gives away their secret animal identity.

OSWALD: What's the mark?

JENNIFER LEIGH: A long, single, hairy eyebrow that extends over both eyes.

OSWALD: *(Elated)* I DON'T HAVE A LONG, SINGLE HAIRY EYEBROW THAT EXTENDS OVER BOTH EYES, HONEY, AND NEITHER DO YOU!!

(The ACTOR *puts the sun down and puts the moon up.)*

JENNIFER LEIGH: Night! We better get back to our well-secured apartment building. We'll come back tomorrow morning and see if we've caught anything.

(They leave.)

*(*YVETTE *comes back on, huffing and puffing.* YVETTE *stops, out of breath.* YVETTE *has a long, single, hairy eyebrow extending over both eyes.)*

YVETTE: Man, I gotta quit running; it's just killing me. It just ain't no substitute for doing the wild thang.

(YVETTE *lights a cigarette. It makes* YVETTE *feel very, very good.*)

(*Suddenly, there's the terrifying sound of a* TIGER *growling, very close.*)

YVETTE: Oh, no. It's that friggin' tiger!

(*The growling gets louder.*)

YVETTE: I run, I'm dead.

(*The growling gets louder still.*)

YVETTE: YOU KEEP AWAY FROM HERE, TIGER!

TIGER: (*Off*) I smell meat!

YVETTE: LEAVE ME ALONE! I EAT A LOT OF JUNKFOOD, AND I TASTE LIKE SHIT!

(*Suddenly,* YVETTE *notices the empty tiger trap and gets an idea.* YVETTE *gets directly under the trap and trips the wire. The trap falls around* YVETTE, *leaving* YVETTE *safely inside.*)

YVETTE: Ha!

(*The* TIGER *enters. The* TIGER *is a huge, impressive beast.*)

TIGER: Where the fuck are ya?!

YVETTE: (*Gleeful*) Here, asshole!

(*The* TIGER *sees* YVETTE *in the cage. The* TIGER *pounces on the cage, rattling it, but the cage is strong and the* TIGER *can't get* YVETTE.)

TIGER: Get outta there!

YVETTE: No way!

(*The* TIGER *gives up rattling the cage. The* TIGER *gives* YVETTE *a dark look.*)

TIGER: Sure you don't wanna come out and PLAY? There are many advantages, you know.

YVETTE: To being eaten by you? Yeah! Right!

TIGER: *(Gentle)* Surely. If I eat you, you won't have to work anymore. You won't have to pay taxes. You'll never have responsibilities. Or tooth decay. You won't have to go through the slow indignity of aging. You won't have to see your parents die, then your brothers and sisters and friends, finally your children. You won't have to pay rent or lug bags of groceries up a dreary eighth-floor walk-up. You won't have to obsess about love and wonder if any person on this earth will ever find you attractive. You won't have to slave away in some airless, colorless, mindless midtown office with eye-bludgeoning incandescent lights shooting into your face. You won't have to fear muggers, their stealthy knives, their bottomless rage. And, best of all, the dreaded uncertainty is over. The terrible tension will be lifted at last. The eternal questions—"when will I die?" "how will I die?"—will be answered. So there's peace in this surrender, my friend. There's courage. Your reward is a quick, painless death—so quick you won't even hear your bones cracking—followed by infinite deep sleep and total incorporation into this exquisite body of mine, as cell by cell I take you over and you become part of my tremendous heart, my lusty musculature, and my excellent mind.

(Beat)

YVETTE: *(A bit hypnotized by this)* Gee...you put it that way....

TIGER: Sounds almost too good to be true, doesn't it?

YVETTE: Uh-huh.

TIGER: So. Open up the cage. Sweetie. And let me in.

(YVETTE starts to open the cage and instantly thinks better of it.)

YVETTE: I love my life! I look forward to old age!

(The TIGER attacks the cage in one last violent burst of fury. But, again, the cage holds and the TIGER is thwarted.)

TIGER: *I don't need you!* There's a lot better meat out there! I could eat the mayor! I could eat the Mets! I COULD EAT A BROADWAY PLAY!

(*The* TIGER *storms off, unhappy growls receding into the distance.*)

(YVETTE *jumps with glee.* YVETTE *waits. Silence.* YVETTE *opens the cage door a crack. We hear a hungry growl, very close.* YVETTE *closes the door fast.*)

YVETTE: Think I'll just spend the night.

(YVETTE *quickly falls asleep, face down.*)

(*The* ACTOR *puts the moon down and puts the sun up.*)

(OSWALD *and* JENNIFER LEIGH *come on, carrying long guns. They creep slowly to the trap.*)

OSWALD: Look!

JENNIFER LEIGH: Eureka!

(*They creep closer. They see* YVETTE, *face down, snoring.*)

OSWALD: *(Disappointed)* It's a jogger.

JENNIFER LEIGH: Great! All that work for nothing! Another night of no sex!

OSWALD: *(To* YVETTE*)* Hey you! Wake up!

(YVETTE *stirs, wakes, sits up yawning, and turns to sleepily face* OSWALD *and* JENNIFER LEIGH.*)

(OSWALD *and* JENNIFER LEIGH *look at* YVETTE *and gasp. They can't believe what they see.*)

JENNIFER LEIGH: Do you see what I see?

YVETTE: 'Sup, y'all!

JENNIFER LEIGH: I SEE A LONG, SINGLE, HAIRY EYEBROW....

OSWALD: ...THAT EXTENDS OVER BOTH EYES!

YVETTE: Did you guys build this thing? It saved my life!

JENNIFER LEIGH: We're going to be the heroes of New York!

YVETTE: I was running through the park last night, minding my own business...

OSWALD: We're going to be responsible for the biggest explosion of sexual activity since the Sixties!

YVETTE: *(Suddenly understanding)* Whoa. Wait. You people don't think I'm the...

JENNIFER LEIGH: *(To* YVETTE*)* Very clever, Tiger. Very clever.

YVETTE: But I'm not the Tiger! I'm Yvette...

(Blam! OSWALD *and* JENNIFER LEIGH *blast* YVETTE *with their guns.* YVETTE *falls over dead. Lots of blood if possible.)*

(Silence. OSWALD *and* JENNIFER LEIGH *look at each other. As fear falls away, an old, primal, irresistible urge takes over.)*

OSWALD: Hi.

JENNIFER LEIGH: Hi.

OSWALD: You, uh...feel anything yet?

JENNIFER LEIGH: Starting to.

OSWALD: A little of that crazy fear melting away?

JENNIFER LEIGH: Fear draining out my fingertips.

OSWALD: Cascading out my veins.

JENNIFER LEIGH: Down the sinews of my generous thighs.

OSWALD: Through the canals of my bold and awakening limbs.

*(*OSWALD *and* JENNIFER LEIGH *jump at each other. A few moments of intense mashing.)*

JENNIFER LEIGH: Wait! We have to let the city know what we've done. We have to spread the word.

(They run off hand in hand. Dead YVETTE *lies in the cage.)*

(The ACTOR *puts the sun down and puts the moon up. It's night. Then the* ACTOR *draws a white chalk outline around* YVETTE's *body.)*

(Strange light on YVETTE *as she sits up and looks at the white outline of her dead body on the stage.)*

YVETTE: Well, isn't this just copacetic. Shot in the prime of life. Turned into a lonely and unremembered ghost at such a young age!

(The TIGER *enters, laughing.)*

TIGER: They—hahhahaha!—they shot *you*—hehehehe!—thinking you were me!!!

YVETTE: Just look at my poor, mangled body. Those horny bastards didn't even bury me!

TIGER: I couldn't've planned it better myself!

YVETTE: You could at least show some *respect*, Tiger.

TIGER: This means I'm in the clear! The city thinks I'm dead! Everyone's guard will be down! This could be the greatest feeding night of my career!

YVETTE: I DESERVE BETTER THAN THIS, TIGER!

(The TIGER *looks at* YVETTE, *tries not to laugh.)*

YVETTE: Death is terrible and lonely, Tiger!

TIGER: Hey, that's life in the big city, Jogger Lady. Wrong place at the wrong time.

YVETTE: Death is cold and sad, Tiger!

TIGER: Law o' the jungle, dude.

YVETTE: Death has kissed me hard and deep, Tiger...and now we're in bed, he and I, making eternal, sad, cold, terrible, and lonely love.

TIGER: I can't listen to this shit! I've got work to do!

(With a blood-curdling roar, the TIGER *bounds off the stage, leaving* YVETTE *alone.)*

(Lights up on an apartment. OSWALD *and* JENNIFER LEIGH *are in bed. They've just made love. They're smoking. The* TIGER *appears at their window.)*

OSWALD: Happy? Satisfied?

JENNIFER LEIGH: Hmmmmmmmmmm. You?

OSWALD: Hmmmmmmmmmm. Yes!

(YVETTE *watches this scene from the cage. The* TIGER *rattles the bars on the windows.*)

TIGER: Hey, you two! It's me! GROWL. It's your worst nightmare! I SAID GROWL.

(OSWALD *and* JENNIFER LEIGH *glance up at the* TIGER, *then resume their conversation as if the* TIGER *weren't there.*)

OSWALD: *(To* JENNIFER LEIGH*)* You know what I enjoy most about making love?

JENNIFER LEIGH: Chronologically, alphabetically, or by subject category?

OSWALD: It's so much like death.

YVETTE: *(Laughing)* It ain't over yet, Tiger! People are pretty fucking funny, you know!

JENNIFER LEIGH: *(To* OSWALD*)* What do you mean, dear?

TIGER: Hey, you! It's me! The tiger! Get outta bed already! Get scared!

OSWALD: It's real and subjective...it's dark and light...it's brief and eternal all at the same time.

TIGER: Hey, what's with you two?! Run for it! Scream! At least make it interesting!

JENNIFER LEIGH: I'm sorry I was ever afraid.

OSWALD: I'll never be afraid again.

(*They kiss, turning their backs on the dumbfounded* TIGER. *Lights down on the apartment.*)

(YVETTE *laughs as the confused and frightened* TIGER *approaches the cage.*)

YVETTE: What's the matter, Tiger?

TIGER: The whole city thinks I'm dead. They're not afraid. They're all *relaxed*. They're all lying around, the entire city of New York, millions and millions having wild sex in their beds and on their floors and on their tabletops and in their elevators and out on their fire escapes! Two by two! Three by three in some areas of Brooklyn! *(Beat. A terrible shudder goes through the* TIGER's *body.)* Nobody's coming out of their homes. Nobody's walking the streets or taking the subways. No one's going to work anymore. I can't get *at* them. I can't get any food! MY STOMACH IS SHRINKING FAST!

YVETTE: Tsk. Tsk.

TIGER: I'm starving! I'm like a shark! Eat constantly or die!

YVETTE: Law o' the jungle, huh?

TIGER: *You did this to me, Jogger Lady! You did this!*

YVETTE: Welcome to death.

TIGER: *(Clutching stomach, starting to die)* I don't wanna die! It's nasty!

(As YVETTE *watches the* TIGER *writhe in agony,* YVETTE *becomes suddenly very sad and pitying.)*

YVETTE: You're right. You're gonna hate it. Come on, Tiger. There's no avoiding it. It's time to make love with the infinite.

*(*YVETTE *opens the cage. The* TIGER *walks in.)*

(The TIGER *and* YVETTE *lie next to each other in the cage. The* TIGER *sobs.* YVETTE *gently puts an arm around the* TIGER*.)*

*(*YVETTE *kisses the* TIGER*, and the* TIGER *dies. The* ACTOR *draws a chalk outline around the* TIGER's *body.)*

(The apartment lights come up as OSWALD *and* JENNIFER LEIGH *have a languid and wonderful orgasm. It's joined by the joyous orgasms of millions of liberated New Yorkers.)*

(Their laughter fills the theater.)

END OF ACT ONE

ACT TWO

GAS

CHARACTER & SETTING

CHEO

TIME

Start of the ground offensive of the Persian Gulf War

PLACE

A gas station

For Juan Carlos Rivera

(*A car at a gas station.* CHEO *stands next to the pump, about to fill his car with gas. He is a working-class Latino. Before he pumps gas he speaks to the audience.*)

CHEO: My brother's letters were coming once a week. I could feel his fear. It was in his handwriting. He sat in a tank. In the middle of the Saudi Arabian desert. Wrote six, seven, eight hours a day. These brilliant letters of fear.

This big Puerto Rican guy! What the fuck's he *doing* out there? What the fucking hell sense *that* make? He's out there, in the Saudi sand, writing letters to me about how he's gonna die from an Iraqi fucking missile. And he's got all this time on his hands to think about his own death. And there's nothing to do 'cause of these restrictions on him. No women, no magazines, 'cause the Saudis are afraid of the revolutionary effects of ads for women's lingerie on the population! Allah would have a cow! There's nothing he's allowed to eat even *remotely* reminds him of home. Nothing but the fucking time to sit and think what it's gonna be like to have some fucking towelhead—as he calls them—run a bayonet clean through his guts. He's sitting in the tank playing target practice with the fucking camels. Shooting at the wind. The sand in all the food. Sand in his dreaming. He and his buddies got a camel one day. They shaved that motherfucker clean! Completely shaved its ass! Then they spray-painted the name of their company, in bright American spray-paint, on the side of the camel, and sent it on its way! Scorpion fights in the tents! All those scenes from fucking *Apocalypse Now* in his head. Fucking Marlon Brando decapitating that guy and Martin Sheen going fucking nuts. That's what fills my brother's daily dreams as he sits out there in the desert, contemplating his own death. The Vietnam Syndrome those people are trying to eradicate. His early letters were all about that. A chronicle. His way of laying it all down, saying it all for me, so I would know what his last days, and months, and seconds were like. So when he got offed by an Iraqi missile, I would at least know what it was like to be in his soul, if just for a little while.

He couldn't write to save his life at first. Spelled everything totally, unbelievably wrong. "Enough": e-n-u-f. "Thought": t-h-o-t. "Any": e-n-y. But with time, he started to write beautifully. This angel started to come out of the desert. This singing angel of words. Thoughts I honestly never knew he had. Confessions. Ideas. We started to make *plans*. We started to be in sync for the first time since I stopped telling him I loved him. I used to kick his fucking ass! It wasn't hard or nothing. That's not bragging, just me telling you a simple truth. He was always sick. Always the first to cry. He played drums in a parade back home. He couldn't even *play* the fucking instrument, he was so uncoordinated. Spastic. But they let him march in the parade anyway—without drumsticks. He was the last guy in the parade, out of step, banging make-believe drum sticks, phantom rhythms on this snare drum— playing *air* drum for thousands of confused spectators! Then he got into uniforms and the scouts. But I knew that bullshit was just a cover anyway. He didn't mean it. Though after he joined the army and was in boot camp, he took particular delight in coming home and demonstrating the fifty neat new ways he learned to kill a guy. One day he forgot he weighed twice my weight and nearly snapped my spine like a fucking cucumber! I thought, in agony, "Where's my bro? Where's that peckerhead I used to kick around? The first one to cry when he saw something beautiful. The first one to say "I love that" or "I love Mom" or "I love you". He never got embarrassed by that, even after I got too old to deal with my fucking little brother kissing me in front of other people. Even later, he always, always, always ended every conversation with, "I love you, bro", and I couldn't say, "I love you", back, 'cause I was too hip to do that shit.

But he got deeper in it. The war thing. He wrote to say I'd never understand. He's fighting for my right to say whatever I want. To disagree. And I just fucking love how they tell you on the news the fucking temperature in Riyadh, Saudi Arabia! Like I fucking care! And a couple of times the son-of-a-bitch called me collect from Saudi! *I said collect!* And I told him if Saddam Hussein didn't kill him, I would! He told me about troubles with his wife back home. He'd just gotten married a month before shipping out. He didn't really know her and was wondering if she still loved him. My brother always loved ugly women. It was a thing with him. Low self-esteem or something. Like he couldn't love himself and didn't understand a woman that would. So he sought out the absolute losers of the planet: trucker whores with prison records who liked to tie him up and whip him, stuff like that. I honestly have trouble contemplating my little brother being whipped by some trucker whore in leather. Love! He didn't know another way. Then he met a girl who on their first date confessed she hated spiks—so my brother married her! This racist looked him in the eye, disrespected his whole race to his face, and my brother says, "I do."

Last night somebody got on T V to say we shouldn't come down on rich people, 'cause rich people are a minority too, and coming down on them was a form of racism! And I thought, they're fucking afraid of class warfare, and they should be! And the news showed some little white punk putting up flags all over this dipshit town in California, and this little twerp's story absorbed *twenty minutes* of the news—this little, blond kid with a smile full of teeth and the protests got shit. And this billboard went up in my town, showing Stalin, Hitler, and Hussein, saying we stopped him twice before we have to stop him again! This billboard was put up by a local newspaper! The music, the computer graphics, the generals coming out of retirement to become media stars, public hard-ons. And we gotta fight NAKED AGGRESSION—like this asshole president should come *to my fucking neighborhood* if he wants to see naked aggression! I never thought the ideas in the head of some politician would mean the death of my brother and absolutely kill my mother. I'm telling you, that woman will not survive the death of my brother no matter how much she believes in God, no matter how much praying she does.

But I keep that from him. I write back about how it's not going to be another Vietnam. It's not going to be a whole country that spits on you when you come back. That we don't forget the ones we love and fight for us. Then his letters stopped. I combed the newspapers trying to figure out what's going on over there, 'cause his letters said nothing about where he was. He wasn't allowed to talk about locations, or troop size, or movement, 'cause, like, I was going to personally transmit this information to the Iraqi fucking Ministry of Defense! I thought about technology. The new shit Iraq has that was made in the United States, shit that could penetrate a tank's armor and literally travel through the guts of a tank, immolating every living human soul inside, turning human Puerto Rican flesh into hot screaming soup, the molecules of my brother's soul mixing with the metal molecules of the iron coffin he loved so much. I couldn't sleep. My mother was suicidal. Why wasn't he writing? The air war's continuing. They're bombing the shit out of that motherfucking country! And I find myself ashamed. I think, "Yeah, bomb it more. Level it. Send it back to the Stone Age. Make it so every last elite Republican Guard is dead. So my brother won't get killed." For the first time in my life, I want a lot of people I don't hate to die, 'cause I know one of them could kill the man I love most in this fucked-up world. If my brother is killed, I will personally take a gun and blow out the brains of George Herbert Walker Bush. And I'm sick. I'm sick of rooting for the bombs. Sick of loving every day the air war continues. Sick of every air strike, every sortie. And being happy another Iraqi tank got taken out and melted, another Iraqi bunker was bombed, another bridge can't bring ammunition, can't deliver that one magic bullet that will incapacitate my brother, bring him back a vegetable, bring him back dead in his soul, or blinded, or butchered in some Iraqi concentration camp. That the Iraqi motherfucker that would torture him won't live now, 'cause our smart bombs have killed that towelhead motherfucker in his sleep! They actually got me wanting this war to be bloody!

Last night the ground war started. It started. The tanks are rolling. I find my gut empty now. I don't have thoughts. I don't have dreams. My mother is a shell. She has deserted herself and left behind a blathering cadaver, this pathetic creature with rosary beads in her hands, looking up to Christ, and C N N, saying words like "Scud," "strategic interests," "collateral damage," "target-rich environment", words this woman from a little town in Puerto Rico has no right to know. So I fight my demons. I think of the cause. Blood for oil. I NEED MY CAR, DON'T I? I NEED MY CAR TO GET TO WORK SO I CAN PAY THE RENT AND NOT END UP A HOMELESS PERSON! DON'T I HAVE A RIGHT TO MY CAR AND MY GAS? AND WHAT ABOUT FREEING DEMOCRATIC KUWAIT?!

So I wait for a sign, anything, a prayer, any sign, I'll take it. Just tell me he's okay. Tell me my brother's gonna kill well and make it through this alive. He's gonna come home and he's gonna come home the same person he left: the spastic one who couldn't spell...the one who couldn't play the drums.

(CHEO *starts to pump gas. As he pumps the gas, he notices something. He pulls the nozzle out of the car. Blood comes out of the gas pump.* CHEO *stares and stares at the bloody trickle coming out of the gas pump.*)

(*Blackout*)

END OF PLAY

THE CROOKED CROSS

CHARACTERS & SETTING

MIRIAM
FOOGMAN
DAN
CHLOE
BLUE EYES
KATHY FOUKES

TIME

The present

PLACE

An American town

(Leather-jacketed MIRIAM *and her leather-jacketed boyfriend* FOOGMAN *are kissing. He wants more. She won't give it to him. She diplomatically pulls free of him.)*

FOOGMAN: Happy birthday.

MIRIAM: C'mon, you better go!

*(*FOOGMAN *laughs. He stops kissing her. He gives her a charismatic smile. Pulls a small, single rose and a candy bar out of his pocket.)*

FOOGMAN: Happy birthday.

(She's stunned. Laughs, surprised, delighted)

MIRIAM: Foogman! You fuck!

(He gives her the rose and candy. He clicks his fingers. Upbeat rock music plays. Laughing, they dance. They hold each other. They laugh.)

(They stop dancing. FOOGMAN *looks at her, reaches into a pocket and pulls out a little black box. When he gives her the box, the music stops.)*

(Delighted beyond words, she opens the little box.)

(There are little silver earrings inside the box in the shape of swastikas. She's taken aback and doesn't respond.)

FOOGMAN: Like it?

MIRIAM: It's.

FOOGMAN: Earrings.

MIRIAM: Swastikas. These are little. Swa—

FOOGMAN: Got 'em in the city. It was easy. But I wanted the best. These. *Pure silver.*

MIRIAM: Were they...expensive?

FOOGMAN: Uh-huh! I think they look cool!

MIRIAM: My father will fucking freak.

FOOGMAN: Good. Put 'em on. I wanna see with this jacket.

MIRIAM: Maybe not. Yet.

FOOGMAN: C'mon, don't you like 'em?

MIRIAM: Sure...

FOOGMAN: Well, do it. They're cool. I mean, what, you don't want them? You don't love me?

MIRIAM: Sure I do. Of course. Hey.

FOOGMAN: They make you different. Hard. Fuck everybody. These are a statement. *Who you are.* You are for me. *That's* what this is, Miriam.

MIRIAM: Isn't there another way I could be for you?

(He takes them back. He starts walking away from her.)

MIRIAM: *Hey...*

FOOGMAN: Fuck you.

MIRIAM: I want them.

(He looks at her.)

MIRIAM: I want them. I do want them. Let me have them. I'll wear them.

FOOGMAN: I said fuck—

MIRIAM: No. For real. Let me. C'mon, don't be like this. It's my birthday. I love them. They're from you, and I love them.

FOOGMAN: Swastikas: oooooooooh...

MIRIAM: They don't mean that. They mean I love you.

FOOGMAN: Never bought you anything before...

MIRIAM: I know this is a big thing for you.

FOOGMAN: You saying I'm cheap?

MIRIAM: I'm saying you're sweet. And nobody knows you like I do. And I really appreciate the gift.

FOOGMAN: Yeah.

MIRIAM: So give it to me.

FOOGMAN: *(Smiles)* I'll give it to you.

(FOOGMAN *kisses her aggressively. Tries to slide his hand between her legs. She pulls back. He hands the earrings back to her. She puts them on.)*

(The second they are on, something strange happens to the lights, like we've just entered an alternate reality. This change is NOT SUBTLE. Neither MIRIAM *nor* FOOGMAN *seem to notice the changes, though* MIRIAM *gets a very strange feeling in the pit of her stomach.)*

(A tall, handsome stranger with BLUE EYES *appears far upstage.)*

*(*FOOGMAN *smiles at* MIRIAM*.)*

FOOGMAN: Kiss.

(Distracted, she kisses him. He gives her an odd look.)

MIRIAM: What's the matter?

FOOGMAN: Where the fuck is your mind?

*(*FOOGMAN *swats her on the ass and swaggers away. He remains onstage, facing the audience with a defiant look.)*

*(*MIRIAM *turns. Walks to her home. Her father* DAN *is watching T V. Before* MIRIAM *approaches* DAN*, she takes off the earrings. The T V laugh track is too loud.)*

MIRIAM: Dad, I got a really weird present from Foogman. I kinda like it, I think.

DAN: Happy birthday.

MIRIAM: He's so interesting. So intense. I really like him.

DAN: There's a chicken pot pie in the oven.

MIRIAM: You know, he tells me these stories about. Like when he got beaten. His uncle tried to rape him. A gang

beat his brother almost to death in front of him.
He only recently started to tell me. The first time,
I couldn't believe it. I understood so much. I mean,
how could any kid live through that?

DAN: We all have our problems, Miriam. We're going
to set up an appointment to get you fitted for birth
control.

(Beat)

MIRIAM: That's not why I'm telling you this.

DAN: We'll do it now, before it's too late.

MIRIAM: I'm telling you about something. Deeper.
About me. I'm not saying, "I wanna fuck my new
boyfriend, do you mind?"

DAN: You are, but you don't know it.

MIRIAM: That's... Dad...why does everything have to be
so cheap? Everything with you, it's either a joke or it's
filthy—

DAN: We'll go Friday.

MIRIAM: I love him, Dad, and he's not going away,
and there's nothing you can do about it!

DAN: There's a box of condoms on your bed, Miriam,
happy birthday.

*(MIRIAM angrily, tearfully, leaves DAN. DAN stays onstage
watching the T V. MIRIAM looks at the earrings. Trembling,
she puts them on.)*

(There's a screaming school bell.)

*(FOOGMAN and MIRIAM go to school. They sit at desks,
holding hands. FOOGMAN is extremely proud that MIRIAM
is wearing the earrings. MIRIAM is defiant.)*

*(KATHY FOUKES enters and takes a seat behind MIRIAM.
She looks at MIRIAM's earrings in horror. MIRIAM smiles
at KATHY. They used to be friends.)*

MIRIAM: Hey, Kathy. How you been? Heard you were sick. You okay now? Listen, I shouldda called you back....

(KATHY *can't answer.*)

(MIRIAM's *teacher* CHLOE *enters and stares at* MIRIAM, *dumbfounded.*)

CHLOE: Miriam. What are you wearing?

MIRIAM: Uh...clothes?

(*Loud canned laughter from the class. Silence from* KATHY.)

CHLOE: Take them off.

MIRIAM: My clothes? What are you, perverted?

(*More canned laughter, louder*)

CHLOE: The earrings, Miriam. Take them *off.*

(*Beat*)

MIRIAM: No.

(*Beat*)

CHLOE: See me after class.

(*The class bell rings, louder than before. The sound of students' chatter, loud, then fading to silence as the class empties.* KATHY *leaves.* CHLOE *turns to* FOOGMAN.)

CHLOE: Get out of here. This isn't about you.

FOOGMAN: I gave her those earrings, Chloe.

MIRIAM: (*To* FOOGMAN) Foog, it's okay....

FOOGMAN: You're not going to make her take them off.

CHLOE: (*To* FOOGMAN) I want you to leave the room, please.

MIRIAM: (*To* FOOGMAN) I can handle this. Just wait for me outside.

FOOGMAN: (*To* CHLOE) C'mon, Chloe. Throw me out. Let's see you throw me out.

MIRIAM: *(To* FOOGMAN*)* WAIT OUTSIDE FOR ME. Wait outside for me. Just wait outside for me. C'MON—YOU DON'T OWN ME—JUST GO!

FOOGMAN: *(To* CHLOE*)* It's the freedom of *expression*. It's the First *Amendment*.

(FOOGMAN *goes into the hallway, staying onstage, facing the audience.* CHLOE *looks at* MIRIAM*, who won't meet* CHLOE*'s eyes.)*

CHLOE: Miriam, you're much too smart. You know what you're wearing. You know what that is.

MIRIAM: Earrings?

CHLOE: DON'T PLAY STUPID. I don't play that with you. I have never treated you stupid. You are not stupid.

MIRIAM: ...I'm going to be late for my next class?

CHLOE: You're not going to wear those earrings in this school. They are an offense. You cheapen yourself. It's amazing you've gotten this far, to third period, without someone beating the living shit out of you. You have nice friends; I can't believe any of them let you get away with this.

MIRIAM: I don't have friends. Anymore. I have him.

(CHLOE *makes a move toward* MIRIAM*.)*

MIRIAM: *You come near me and I'll fucking have you fired and don't think I won't!*

(CHLOE *stops. Beat)*

CHLOE: Look. I am Jewish. Do you know what it does to me to see that on your body? Do you understand how my gut feels?

MIRIAM: What does that have anything to do with it?

CHLOE: DON'T PLAY GAMES WITH ME FOR GODSAKES!

(Beat)

MIRIAM: I'm not. I'm not.

CHLOE: The Nazis killed Jews! Six million of us! Don't you fucking know *anything*?!

MIRIAM: ...They did? *(Beat)* Okay. So now I know! But wasn't that a long time ago? Before I was born? Before my *mother*? That was a different time. A different world. Didn't all those guys die on D-Day or something? All you Jews are okay now. You have houses. You have stuff. Nobody's going to kill you ever again. That shit is over. It's behind us. Get over it. This is just jewelry. It's just a shape. It's a dead thing, Chloe. It's not a threat. It's just a piece of silver in a crooked cross. It's cool. A lot of kids wear them, pins, medallions, the rebels, and I identify with that. I have my own mind, and I know what I think, and I know I don't hate Jews—like, wasn't Kathy Foukes one of my best *friends*?—so I can wear whatever I want, and it doesn't mean *shit*, it's only *clothing*.

(MIRIAM *gets up to go.* CHLOE *grabs her.* MIRIAM *screams. They struggle. Shaking, angry,* MIRIAM *pulls out a knife and slashes at* CHLOE. CHLOE *backs away.*)

(*Angry and afraid,* MIRIAM *leaves* CHLOE. CHLOE *angry, impotent, stays onstage, facing the audience.*)

(MIRIAM *runs to* FOOGMAN. FOOGMAN *speaks to the audience.*)

FOOGMAN: I'm bleeding on the inside. No one knows my true insides. No one sees my bleeding organs. Like some god wired me all wrong, sewed me together with barbed wire, connected my lungs to my heart to my guts to my fucking mind with thorns of iron instead of flesh: And that's what's keeping me alive and killing me all at the same time.

(FOOGMAN *repeats the speech, low, as* MIRIAM *leaves* FOOGMAN *and goes to* DAN.)

DAN: There's a chicken pot pie in the oven. I've made over fifty thousand of them. They come individually wrapped. You preheat the oven. Three hundred and fifty degrees Fahrenheit. Then you put the frozen pie in the oven and cook for thirty minutes. My family owns eleven hundred buttons. I have prepared nine acres of Jello.

(DAN *and* FOOGMAN *repeat their speeches, low, as* MIRIAM *goes to* CHLOE.)

CHLOE: I went to Harvard! What the fuck am I doing here? What the fuck am I doing here? What the fuck am I doing here? What the fuck am I doing here? What the fuck am I doing here?

(CHLOE, FOOGMAN, *and* DAN *stop speaking at the same time. They leave the stage together. Silence*)

(MIRIAM *is alone for a second. As* BLUE EYES *goes to her, he changes the lighting on the stage.*)

BLUE EYES: I have interesting teeth. They are straight and white, and each individual tooth is perfectly square.

MIRIAM: Yeah?

BLUE EYES: My hair is easy to comb. The part in my hair is a straight line. You might even describe that part in my hair as "razor straight."

MIRIAM: *(Tentative smile)* That's very interesting.

(MIRIAM *starts to go.*)

BLUE EYES: Don't go. I'm new in town. I don't have any friends.

MIRIAM: Yeah. Well. What can I tell you?

BLUE EYES: Don't you think my eyes are very blue?

(*She hesitates—then looks. His eyes are beautiful, hypnotic. But she's still fighting them.*)

MIRIAM: Yes. Yes, blue.

BLUE EYES: My eyes are the purest blue. My heart is pure too. My heart is full of love.

MIRIAM: "My heart is full of love." You don't hear people talk like that too much. "My heart is full of love." It's—it's—weird... *(Beat)* It's nice.

BLUE EYES: I'm new in town. I don't have any friends.

MIRIAM: *(Weakening)* Yeah...well...that'll change. Especially with that face of yours, those eyes...

BLUE EYES: My heart is wide and generous as the sea. My heart has room for the good people of the world. The good people. My heart weeps for the weak and defenseless. There is no hypocrisy in my heart, only passion and truth. I have learned to tame my heart. In order to spare my heart the unbelievable pain that comes with life, I've taught it to beat on command. When I tell my heart to stop, it stops. The blood stops flowing. It rests in the iron cradles of my veins. Waiting patiently there for the next command. My blood will not surge for the undeserving. It will not make its pretty drum music for the bad people of our world. No, it will not do that. *(Beat)* I like your taste in jewelry.

MIRIAM: The earrings? You're the only one....

BLUE EYES: That's too bad. You're a girl after my own heart, as they say. *(He gets closer to her. Beat.)* A lot of people should be ashamed the way they treat you! I bet they don't care what you have to say—and you have a lot to say! No...there's so much inside you... so much life, beauty, even anger and savagery...and they don't even know, do they? Fuckers! I hate them! You got a boyfriend?

MIRIAM: *(Flirtatious)* Um. Well...not any more...

BLUE EYES: *(Smiles)* There's going to be a party tonight. Some friends. At my house. Would you like to come?

MIRIAM: A party? I thought you said you didn't have friends...

BLUE EYES: Just some like-minded folk who don't like what's going on and want to change it. I think you'll like them. I know they'll like you. There'll be music!

(A waltz plays. Lights change to ballroom lighting. BLUE EYES takes the amazed MIRIAM in his arms, and they waltz merrily around the stage. At first it's fun. MIRIAM is laughing. But soon it's violent. MIRIAM is uncomfortable and finally pulls free.)

(The music stops. BLUE EYES looks at her, hurt.)

BLUE EYES: What's the matter? I'm not used to being around a pretty girl. I make mistakes. I try not to, but with you any man would be nervous!

MIRIAM: No, it's just. I'm not. Much for parties 'n shit.

(Slight beat. The lighting returns to normal.)

BLUE EYES: I understand. We'll speak again?

MIRIAM: Um.

BLUE EYES: Promise me, Miriam. Promise me we'll speak again.

(BLUE EYES kisses MIRIAM on both ears. His hot breath enters her ears—it's delicious and terrifying—and she almost gasps. He goes away and stands onstage, facing the audience.)

MIRIAM: I promise.

(MIRIAM, a little rattled by BLUE EYES's visit, starts to take off the earrings.)

(They won't come off. She tries to pull them, harder. Still, they won't come off. MIRIAM starts to panic. She pulls so hard she's starting to hurt herself.)

MIRIAM: C'mon, you fucks—ow!—shit!

(There's an explosion. Suddenly, the stage is bathed in bright red light. There are screams—like the collective screams of millions of people. MIRIAM has to cover her eyes. Distant sirens mingle with the screams. FOOGMAN runs up to MIRIAM. They have to shout over the horrible noise.)

FOOGMAN: You gotta see this! THEY BLEW UP A HOUSE!

MIRIAM: What house? Who did?

FOOGMAN: Nazis! Nazis! Blew up Kathy Foukes's house to fucking pieces! Painted big swastikas all over the fucking street! I couldn't believe it!

MIRIAM: ...Kathy? Is Kathy okay?

FOOGMAN: She's dead! The whole family's dead! I've never seen anything like it! I've never seen an explosion like that! Kathy and her whole family, blown up, flames, smoke, screaming! They pulled the bodies out! They're all black! The firemen are puking! Everyone's crying! It's amazing!

MIRIAM: Oh, my God.

FOOGMAN: Wanna go see it, it's still burning!

MIRIAM: No!

FOOGMAN: Everyone's there!

MIRIAM: No! I don't want to! You're sick!

FOOGMAN: C'mon! You pissed at me or something?

MIRIAM: How can you think about something like that? Kathy Foukes and her whole family have been burned alive! How could you think about anything else?

FOOGMAN: You know? I'm outta here! You're a fucking psycho! Fucking inconsistent bitch psycho!

(FOOGMAN *leaves.* MIRIAM *starts to cry.*)

MIRIAM: Oh, my God. Kathy.

(BLUE EYES *enters, laughing, carrying a dozen roses and a box of candy. The noise instantly stops. Silence, except for the laughter.*)

BLUE EYES: Hey, gorgeous—hey, beautiful, I think I'm in love with you! I think I want you to meet my mother!

(MIRIAM *controls her crying and looks at* BLUE EYES.
He laughs so hard, he falls to the ground and rolls around, laughing.)

MIRIAM: ...Was it you?

BLUE EYES: I really want to make love with you!
I really want to know you in the biblical sense!
I really wanna fuck your brains out, Miriam!

MIRIAM: It was, wasn't it?

(BLUE EYES *stops laughing. He stands up and looks at* MIRIAM.)

(*He signals for the waltz music to begin. It does.*
BLUE EYES *approaches* MIRIAM *and starts to undress.*)

BLUE EYES: Somebody so young. So strong.
Good womb. An entire future in front of her.
There she is! Proudly displaying her unique
and terrifying orthodoxy!

MIRIAM: Why? Why did you motherfuckers kill Kathy Foukes?

BLUE EYES: Welcome...

(*He goes to her, shirtless, holding out the flowers and candy. She backs away, trembling.*)

MIRIAM: But I'm not one of you. I'm not. I'm me.
I'm just me. I'm just a person. I'm a person living
in this town and I go to school and I *have* a boyfriend
and I do certain things and those things are who I am,
and maybe they're not too smart, but that's tough shit,
'cause mainly it's *harmless*, 'CAUSE I KNOW WHO
YOU ARE AND I AM NOT ONE OF YOU.

BLUE EYES: Take off the earrings if you're not one of us.

(*Beat*)

MIRIAM: I. I can't. They won't come off.

BLUE EYES: *(Laughing)* They won't come off! Why? Do they have a mind of their own? Are they stuck to you like magic?

MIRIAM: Yes. Like. Magic.

BLUE EYES: *(Laughing)* You shouldn't lie to yourself! Come on. Come. Hold me. Hold me. Come on. Fuck me. Come on, bitch. Fuck me. Hold me! Suck me! Suck me! You wanna suck me!

(BLUE EYES *embraces* MIRIAM. *She screams and tries to fight him off. He succeeds at tearing some of her clothes. She pulls free and falls to the ground.*)

(*Crying, shaking, hurt, humiliated, she lies on the ground.* BLUE EYES *looks at her, smiles. He signals for the music to stop. He throws the roses and the candies on her, then leaves.*)

(*The fire stops. Lights change violently.* MIRIAM *gasps.*)

(KATHY *enters, dressed like a Nazi concentration camp prisoner. Her costume must be as authentic and truthful as possible: the shorn head, tattoo, etc.* MIRIAM *looks at* KATHY *in silence.*)

MIRIAM: Kathy?

KATHY: Hey, Mir'.

MIRIAM: Is it true?

KATHY: Yep. Ka-BOOM.

MIRIAM: Oh, God.

KATHY: I was in the middle of math homework. I was trying to understand the square root of negative one when it happened. I was totally stuck. I still have no idea what it is. Do you?

(Beat)

MIRIAM: It's. It's imaginary. You know. An imaginary number.

KATHY: Can they do that? Can they make that up?

MIRIAM: I don't know.

KATHY: You have a problem in math you can't solve, but you *have* to, or else the whole bullshit crumbles, so you solve it by *making up a fucking imaginary number*?!

MIRIAM: Guess so.

KATHY: Now, if I did that. In real life. I'd get shit for it. They'd call it cheating.

MIRIAM: I guess you won't have to worry about that anymore.

KATHY: I guess not. Guess I won't have to worry about handing in my homework late. Or never figuring out how to use an imaginary number.

MIRIAM: Did it hurt? Did it burn?

KATHY: No. Only, I guess, the *force*. I felt some of the force. Like a strong wind. I felt myself lifted by this strong wind shooting through the kitchen. But no heat or nothing. No pain.

MIRIAM: *(About to cry)* Oh, God. I'm going to miss you!

(MIRIAM *cries long and hard.* KATHY *looks at her.*)

KATHY: Why? Didn't you hate me too?

MIRIAM: No, I would never hate you....

KATHY: But those earrings. Your friends.

MIRIAM: They don't mean anything! When are people going to stop it with the fucking earrings! They are meaningless!

(KATHY *smiles sadly.*)

(KATHY *touches* MIRIAM *on the ears and the earrings fall instantly to the ground.* MIRIAM *sighs with relief.* KATHY *picks up the earrings.*)

(KATHY *hands the earrings back to* MIRIAM. MIRIAM *looks at the silver swastikas.*)

MIRIAM: But they're meaningless, Kathy. They really are.

KATHY: Goodbye.

(KATHY *slowly starts to disappear.* MIRIAM *screams to* KATHY.)

MIRIAM: They are meaningless! JESUS, THEY ARE!!

KATHY: I'm sorry.

(KATHY *is gone.*)

(*The stage darkens abruptly.* MIRIAM *gasps. In the dark,* MIRIAM *sobs uncontrollably.*)

MIRIAM: Don't leave me alone! You asshole! You shit! I don't know where everybody is! I don't know where I am now! Where's my father! Where's my boyfriend! I don't wanna be alone here! They're meaningless! Meaningless! Meaningless!

(*The waltz music returns, distorted. Instant blackout.*)

(*In the black,* MIRIAM *screams. Then there's silence.*)

END OF PLAY

THE WINGED MAN

CHARACTERS & SETTING

Daysi
The Winged Man
Wanda
Allysha

TIME

The present

PLACE

A suburb

1

(*A cave. Very dark.* DAYSI *is entering the cave with her flashlight. She's a young high school student exploring the cave for her geology class. She stops, looks around, and makes a few notes in her notebook. She hears a groan. She stops writing and looks around. The groaning stops. She wants to get out of there—but her fear is overcome by her curiosity. The groaning starts. She follows the sound.*)

(*Lights up on another part of the cave. We see a thin, naked,* WINGED MAN *with large, bloodied wings lying on the ground. There's a bullet hole in the* WINGED MAN's *chest, and only his hand against the blood hole keeps him from bleeding to death. One of his beautiful wings is badly broken. A pool of blood covers the cave floor. The* WINGED MAN *groans.*)

(*The light from* DAYSI's *flashlight rakes the cave floor and comes to rest on the* WINGED MAN. DAYSI *screams and drops the flashlight. She picks it up. She looks at the* WINGED MAN. *He isn't moving. His eyes are closed. It's hard to tell if he's dead or alive.*)

(DAYSI *approaches the* WINGED MAN *cautiously. She bends down and very carefully touches his wings. The* WINGED MAN *groans weakly. She gasps. She steps back. And then forward. She bends down again. Touches the* WINGED MAN's *back. Strokes it. The* WINGED MAN *opens his eyes and looks at her. His eyes are beautiful.*)

(*She almost gasps again. Pulls back from him. Then she moves closer.*)

(*Blackout*)

2

(Lights up on the cave. An hour later.)

(The WINGED MAN *is lying with his head propped up against an improvised pillow. A tightly bound white cloth over his chest has stopped his bleeding. A blanket is draped over his nakedness.* DAYSI *is feeding the* WINGED MAN. *He takes the food and chews weakly.* DAYSI *gives him some water. He swallows greedily. He wants more and more. She laughs at his robust thirst.)*

(He looks at her and slowly holds out his hand to DAYSI. *She reaches out her own hand. Their fingers find each other and intertwine. They sit there a moment, just holding each other's hands. He opens his mouth to speak. She's dying to know who he is, what he is. She inches closer to him. A strange guttural sound comes out of the* WINGED MAN. *He seems to be trying to communicate with her but he can't. She tries to understand but she can't. She looks into his strange and troubled eyes. She smiles at his courageous attempt at speech. Suddenly, he is gripped by terrible pain in his chest—over his wound—he screams and screams. It's unbearable to listen to.* DAYSI *does everything she can to calm him, ease his pain, stroking his forehead, kissing him, anything. The terrible pain subsides, and the* WINGED MAN *calms down.* DAYSI *puts both arms around him. They look at each other.)*

(She holds him tight, rocking him back and forth. He cries very quietly. She is overcome with emotion and cries too. She kisses him.)

(Blackout)

3

(Lights up on a kitchen table)

(DAYSI sits at breakfast, wearing a white feather in her hair, staring into space. Her mother WANDA is with her. WANDA doesn't like the way DAYSI looks. They look at each other silently. Something is preying on the girl's mind—but she can't articulate it yet. She starts to tremble. DAYSI calms down and then looks at WANDA.)

DAYSI: I'm pregnant.

(WANDA looks at DAYSI. WANDA slaps DAYSI across the face.)

(Blackout)

(In the blackout, during the scene change, we hear:)

DAYSI'S VOICE: The baby's father. The baby's father is dead. The baby's father was either an angel from Heaven or, more likely, he was, he was of a race of, of winged men, of, of, human people...who...had...wings.

4

(Lights up on a high school hallway. A row of lockers.)

(DAYSI is at her locker. ALLYSHA comes along. ALLYSHA looks at DAYSI, who looks like she has a bad case of morning sickness. DAYSI leans against the locker, very weak, nauseous.)

ALLYSHA: I hear ya got knocked up.

(Beat)

DAYSI: Word travels fast.

(Beat)

ALLYSHA: Okay, who was it, Daysi? For real.

(Beat)

DAYSI: You tell me.

ALLYSHA: Oh, you fucked an *angel*? You expect me to *believe* that? Okay, maybe he was *like* an angel, but come on. Who was it? Carlos? Ramon? Vinnie? Claudio? All of 'em? None of 'em? Were ya doing it all at once with a variety of gentlemen and now ya can't figure out who is the owner of the lucky sperm? I can understand that. But that's not like you, that's like me, or, like, that's what some people *think* of me, but it's not what anyone thinks of *you*, least of all me. Ya know but ya not telling.

DAYSI: I fucked an angel.

ALLYSHA: Oh, come on, Daysi, please, I'm ya best friend already. Ya don't have to play games with me. I've seen it all with ya. I'm cool. I don't judge. I just wanna help. Tell me who it is. You and I will go to this son-of-a-bitch, ask him why he didn't use a condom, then we're gonna shake the bastard down for money for an abortion, now who is he?

DAYSI: I'm having the baby.

ALLYSHA: Ya not having the baby.

DAYSI: It's a miracle baby, Allysha!

ALLYSHA: It's *killing* ya. Look at ya. Ya my best friend, and I don't wanna see ya throw ya life away on some romance, ya much too young to be a mother, ya still a girl yaself, ya told me ya had plans and ya weren't gonna do the same bullshit ya mother did, and now ya telling me *this*? What am I, stupid?

DAYSI: I'm having the baby.

(Beat)

ALLYSHA: Fine. How ya gonna pay for it?

DAYSI: I'll work.

ALLYSHA: At two bucks an hour!? Have ya priced formula? Have ya priced diapers? Get real. Babies are cash *intensive*. Ya on ya own, honey. Ya mother won't put up with having this illegitimate thing in her house—.

DAYSI: It's not a thing. It's a beautiful baby with wings.

(Beat)

ALLYSHA: Great. I'm going to *math*. I have an appointment with REALITY. Ya wanna join me in reality, please call, okay?, ya have the number.

(ALLYSHA *leaves.* DAYSI *puts her hands over her mouth and nearly throws up. She gags, nearly falls over.* ALLYSHA *comes running back on, concerned.)*

ALLYSHA: Hey. I'm sorry. I'm being an asshole. Hey. I love ya. I'm here for ya. Whatever ya want, Daysi. I'm here for ya. A hundred percent. Okay? I love ya. I want ya to be happy. Okay? *(No answer)* I think it's gonna be a beautiful baby.

(DAYSI *smiles weakly and takes* ALLYSHA's *hand.)*

(Blackout)

(In the blackout, during the scene change, we hear:)

DAYSI'S VOICE: I bet he was of this ancient race. That predates us all. That was around from the beginning. From earliest time. And they lived in harmony on the earth for millions of years. And they were happy here. Flying over the virgin world. Swooping, soaring. Secular angels. The source, you know, of our mythology regarding angels. The original vision. These winged people who survived millions of years until our kind came along with sticks and stones, then arrows, and howitzers, with guns and poisons, slowly, efficiently eradicating this magnificent species, killing them all until there was only one left. One.

(Lights up at a park bench)

(DAYSI *is sitting there. She's several months pregnant and showing. She and* ALLYSHA *feed pigeons out of bags of birdseed.* DAYSI *looks radiant, beautiful.*)

ALLYSHA: God, it's a beautiful day, I can't fucking believe it.

DAYSI: *(Feeding)* Here chick chick chick chick chick. Here chick chick.

ALLYSHA: Is that what ya call pigeons? Chick? That don't sound right.

DAYSI: Here chick. Get your lunch.

ALLYSHA: Should be, "Here, ya parasite-ridden flying sacks o' shit". That's more appropriate.

DAYSI: They're not. They're beautiful.

ALLYSHA: To *you*—in *your* condition—*everything* is beautiful.

DAYSI: Chicky chicky chicky.

(Beat)

ALLYSHA: Ya mother says ya don't like to eat eggs anymore.

DAYSI: That's right.

ALLYSHA: Why is that?

DAYSI: Seems like cannibalism.

ALLYSHA: But ya not a bird!

DAYSI: I just don't like it! I see eggs on a dish, that soft yoke, see it punctured by a fork, start to bleed, all that potential lost, I get sad!

ALLYSHA: Ya mother says ya won't eat poultry. She says ya being weird!

DAYSI: Allysh', I'm *happy*. The morning sickness is over. I feel the baby kicking. And I just want to stay *happy*.

ALLYSHA: She says ya built a nest in ya room!

DAYSI: Just a little one.

ALLYSHA: Just a *little* one?! She says it covers your entire bed now, this whole friggin' fuckin' humungus nest with twigs and leaves and—!

DAYSI: I can't help it! It's an impulse! I just did it, that's all!

ALLYSHA: It's not normal. Tell me ya gonna dismantle it. Tell me that right now!

DAYSI: But it's gonna be. The baby's. The baby's nest. The baby's perch. Not a crib. No. He's not getting a crib! He's getting a beautiful, round, perfect nest his father woulda been proud to see!

ALLYSHA: You are. *Persisting.* In this. *Madness.*

DAYSI: It's not. It's not madness. *(Beat)* Let me show you something. Let me show you what nobody knows. I've been working overtime at White Castle so I could make enough money for this 'cause, I know I wouldn't get any from Mom. I went to a radiologist. And I got me a magic picture of the fetus in my womb. *(She reaches into a pocket and pulls out a tiny, fuzzy black and white ultrasound photo.)* Ultrasound. Isn't it a miracle? The one place in your lifetime you're guaranteed privacy, and you can't even get that anymore!
They have cameras that go into the darkness before birth and snap your picture! There he is. There's my baby. There's the son of the winged man.

(DAYSI *gives* ALLYSHA *the picture.*)

DAYSI: Can you see? I know it's fuzzy. But there. A head. Eye holes. Great magnificent brain. Heart, fingers, toes, genitals. And wings. Right there.
Use your God-given eyes, Allysha. Use your eyesight. And check out these fucking beautiful wings on my son.

(ALLYSHA *stares at the picture. She is trying with all her might to see the wings. She finally does. She's shaken. She hands the photo back.*)

ALLYSHA: I don't see a frikkin' thing.

(DAYSI *takes the photo back. She starts to cry.*)

DAYSI: You're just saying that to be mean.

(*The two sit side by side in silence.* DAYSI *wiping her tears.* ALLYSHA *trying to control her shaking and fear.* DAYSI *starts to absently eat the birdseed. She likes the taste of it. She eats more and more, faster and faster,* ALLYSHA *watching her aghast.*)

(*Blackout*)

(*In the blackout, during the scene change, we hear:*)

DAYSI'S VOICE: One single, beautiful man, the last of his kind, shot through the heart by some amazed hunter, some hick with a shotgun with visions of trophies in his head. And he wounded this man, who found a cave to die in, the last of his world, and he was quietly prepared to die there, until. Until me.

(*Lights up on a tree.*)

(DAYSI, *nine months pregnant, sits on the branch of a tree, looking at the birds flying all around her. The sounds of birds fill the air. Wind is blowing and she is enjoying the feeling of rushing air going through her hair.*)

(WANDA *enters.* WANDA *looks up at* DAYSI.)

WANDA: Are you coming down for dinner? Are you going to spend another night in that tree? What's with you? You're going to be a mother any day now. That makes you squarely a woman, Daysi. A woman. WOMAN. Just like me. Once you have this baby, you're going to be no different than me. You'll have passed that borderland, that place in which your childhood is buried forever. You'll have to give up all the trappings of your childhood. You'll never play in the same way. The air in your lungs will never feel the same again. On the other side of the mirror a face will look back at you full of care and sleeplessness and the memory of pain. Now, I can understand you're afraid of that. But you should have thought of that before you got knocked up! Sitting up in a tree all day and night for weeks is not going to change that. It's not going to make the deep responsibility go away. That baby is going to need you desperately. That baby isn't going to want to hear your fantasies about some winged man you had a one-night stand with. It's going to ask hard questions, Daysi. You're going to have to be honest with your baby and with yourself. And that honesty should start today, baby. Today. With you getting down off that tree and cease eating birdseed and dismantling that fucking nest in your bed! Put that fantasy away, child. A boy knocked you up. A real person. Not a miracle. Not fantasy. Get real, baby. Get off that tree. Start living your life.

(WANDA *waits.* DAYSI *opens her mouth and makes the same guttural sounds the* WINGED MAN *had made. The sounds are strange—and they get louder.* WANDA *puts her hands over her ears. The sound of birds fills the theater.*)

(*Blackout*)

(*In the blackout, during the scene change, we hear:*)

DAYSI'S VOICE: Until I came along. And kept him alive for a couple of hours. And fed him. And watched over him. Then finally made love with him, because I knew the line would end if he died, and I wanted a chance to save the species, to keep that race of winged humans alive just a little longer. Through me. What do you think of that?

(*Lights up at the park bench*)

(DAYSI, *no longer pregnant, enters pushing a stroller. We hear a baby crying.* DAYSI *stops pushing the stroller. She looks around to make sure no one is watching her. She reaches into a pocket and takes out a can of worms. She starts feeding the worms, one by one, to the baby. The crying stops.*)

(Short silence)

(Then we hear happy cooing sounds coming from the baby. DAYSI *smiles.)*

DAYSI: Awwwwwwww. Chulo! Cute.

*(*DAYSI *reaches into the stroller. She holds up the bundled baby. She kisses the baby—then throws the bundle in the air.* DAYSI *waves goodbye as the baby flies away.)*

(Blackout)

END OF PLAY

CPSIA information can be obtained
at www.ICGtesting.com
Printed in the USA
LVHW081516010922
727372LV00008B/366